Reality Check:
Teenage Fathers Speak Out

Many young men feel confused about how to deal with the opposite sex.

Reality Check:

Teenage Fathers Speak Out

by Margi Trapani

THE ROSEN PUBLISHING GROUP, INC.

NEW YORK

Published in 1997, 1999 by The Rosen Publishing Group, Inc.
29 East 21st Street, New York, NY 10010

Revised Edition 1999

Library of Congress Cataloging-in-Publication Data

Trapani, Margi.
    Reality check : teenage fathers speak out / by Margi Trapani.
      p. cm. — (The teen pregnancy prevention library)
    Includes bibliographical references and index.
    Summary: Teenage fathers highlight the challenges of being a teen parent, discussing responsibility, economic hardship, and emotional issues involved in parenting at a young age.
    ISBN 0-8239-2995-7
    1. Teenage fathers—United States—Case studies—Juvenile literature. 2. Teenage pregnancy—United States—Case studies—Juvenile literature. [1. Teenage fathers. 2. Parenting.]
I. Title. II. Series.
HQ756.7.T73 1997
306.874'2—dc20   95-42450
                                                CIP
                                                  AC

Manufactured in the United States of America

Contents

Introduction   6

1) Kenyatta—To Give His Son a Different Life   13

2) Michael—Learning About Responsibility   21

3) Zachary—A Daughter Is Very Special   29

4) Alfred—Getting to Know Your Son   39

5) John—Making a Life for a Family of Five   45

Epilogue   55

Glossary   57

Help List   59

For Further Reading   61

Index   63

Introduction

WE ALL HAVE TO MAKE A LOT OF CHOICES IN our lives. From picking our friends to picking our classes, from selecting a sports team to join or root for to finding a job, the decision or choice, for the most part, is left up to us. But what about adulthood? Do we have a choice about becoming adults? According to the law, we all become adults at the age of eighteen, ready or not; boys officially become men and girls officially become women.

Is manhood that easy, though? Do you simply become a man because of your age? Should you already know what it means to be a man when you are in your teens? How do you know when you've really become a man?

Some young men think that getting a girl pregnant and fathering a baby will make them into men. If you think manhood is confusing, though, you can be sure that fatherhood will be even harder. But unlike manhood, as defined by law, there is a big difference with fatherhood: you have

Many teen mothers raise their babies alone or with the help of parents and grandparents.

a choice. You can choose whether or not to become a father. In fact, it is one of the biggest choices you will ever make. You can decide when you want to become a father. It doesn't just happen by accident.

Today in the United States and around the world, teens are faced with a lot of serious and difficult choices and situations. One of the most confusing issues you will face as a teenager is sex and your relationship with a partner. According to a study by the Centers for Disease Control, the majority of teenage students today, for the first time in decades, have made the choice to not be sexually active. Among sexually active students, the majority now regularly use some form of birth control.

Sex education might be one of your most important lessons in becoming a man. Every teenager needs to learn about condoms and other forms of contraception; to learn about abstaining from sex and the power of waiting; and to learn about the ugly reality of sexually transmitted diseases (STDs), especially AIDS, which has led to hundreds of thousands of deaths.

If you don't take time to learn this lesson, to talk to your parents or relatives or counselors or coaches, then you're not preparing to be a man. You also might be in for the biggest and roughest surprise of your life: unplanned fatherhood.

The United States has the highest rate of teen pregnancy and teen births of all of the Western industrialized nations. In fact, nearly one million teens become pregnant each year. Eight out of ten of those pregnancies were not intended, and happened to unwed mothers.

Do only girls get pregnant? Of course. But a man—or maybe even a boy—is the other part of that pregnancy. Unplanned pregnancy is never a "girl's problem." In fact, according to one study, three out of four girls surveyed had sex because their boyfriends wanted them to. And what happened? The majority of sexually active kids, including eight out of ten girls and six out of ten boys, wished they had waited. Why? Perhaps they weren't ready, or they didn't have any special feelings for their partner. Here's another reason: A sexually active teen who does not use birth control has a 90 percent chance of pregnancy within a year. Remember, pregnancy just doesn't happen by accident. But it happens. And it is no game.

For the teenager, your choice to become a father has already begun. You didn't just have sex, after all; you made a baby. This is reality—you are a father. You have brought another child into this world. Even if you still feel like a child yourself, you now have to learn even more quickly about what it means to be a man and a father—a good father.

Many teenage fathers leave before they can learn how to be good men and good fathers. There are many reasons that young fathers give for leaving and abandoning their kids. Some may not be accepted by the baby's mother or her family. Others might be confused about their financial responsibilities toward the baby or their legal rights as fathers. Some may already be overwhelmed by their own lives at school or work. Still others might not even care—just like their own unknown fathers, perhaps—and think they can disappear like ghosts. Those ghosts will always be haunted by the reality of a child who is their son or daughter.

This book is about five teenage fathers who did the right thing. They made the right choice. They decided to become fathers and play an active role in the lives of their children. Some are married, others are not. Every one of them has been forced to deal with the hard realities of raising babies, as well as the hard realities of staying safe, paying bills, and keeping healthy. They have all made major sacrifices they never could have imagined.

What is important is how they continue to seek out and learn the lessons about what it means to be a man and a father. They continue to try to learn how to finish school or pursue a GED and then continue onto college or other training. They are finding out how to juggle a job and other commitments while taking part in the life of their child; how to form a stronger partnership with their wife or girlfriend while growing stronger themselves. They are still learning how to have fun, as teenagers, while realizing the limits of their new world, and how to love their children and treasure the moments of infancy.

The stories told by these five teen fathers and their relationships might sound similar to yours. In fact, while you read these stories, you can think about your own life and your relationships and situation. Try to imagine yourself in their places. What kind of father would you be?

None of the young men who tell their stories in this book believed that parenthood would happen to them when it did. None of them knew how much becoming fathers would change their lives.

You cannot really know what it is like to become a parent until you do so. These five stories, however, are a glimpse into the reality of teen fatherhood.

KENYATTA IS NINETEEN YEARS OLD. HE HAS been involved in the Operation Fatherhood Program in Trenton, New Jersey.

Kenyatta hopes to study for his GED, but he has put his educational goals aside until he has a stable job and can support his family.

1 KENYATTA— To Give His Son a Different Life

I WAS SIXTEEN WHEN MY CHILD, ANDRE, WAS BORN. I have a very good relationship with the mother of my child. I'm seeking employment now, and we hope to get married. I'm waiting until I'm established and have employment. I can take care of my family then.

At first I was nervous and scared, basically because of the input from both of our families. Both of our families were in the church and disapproved of having sex before marriage. I also didn't expect everything to be on me. Now that I'm older, I realize that I'm a man and I should be the head of the family. My girlfriend and I hadn't planned to have a child, but we were in love and we wanted to be together.

I have a pretty good understanding with her family now. However, she's young. When I try to tell her some things she can't do now that she's a mother, it's hard because she thinks I'm trying to tear her down and not letting her have her freedom. Andre is always asking me, "Why is Mommy always running around? Why doesn't she spend more time with me and you, Daddy?" She's not so much going out on dates, but she wants to get to that stage. I'm afraid once she takes that route, she'll just be out there.

I'm looking for a job, something stable, that will make me a career. Maybe I'll work for the state or be a security guard.

I haven't completed high school. I'd rather take care of my son and my girlfriend first, then decide about getting married, and then get a job. After I'm stabilized, I can go to school at night to get my diploma.

My family and I have an understanding, but it's hard. Sometimes Andre cries and wants to be with his mother when he's with us. I think he cries when he just wants her comfort. Sometimes his mother thinks my family is trying to tie her down with him.

I told my girlfriend that even though we're not married, I'll take care of her and Andre. At family court, they don't care that I buy my girlfriend and Andre clothes and stuff like that; they consider those just accessories. All they look at is that child-support payment. So my girlfriend thought I wasn't supporting her and would walk out any day.

Andre lives with my girlfriend, but if I'm not

working or at the Operation Fatherhood Program, then we're together the majority of the time. I'm not the type who wants to be hanging out on the corner. All that most of my associates—I won't call them friends—want to do is hang on the corner. I don't have time for that. I'm closer to the men at the program—we open up there more than we do at home.

My father, my mother, my sisters, and my girlfriend's mother, sisters, and aunts treat Andre like he was their child. Sometimes we have to let them know that we're the parents. He's so young, sometimes he starts to run and bang things up and the relatives just laugh. They think it's funny. I know he's a baby, but he has to know what he can't do, or else when he's older, he'll terrorize people. Now he thinks, "Auntie or Grandma won't stop me." So I have to stop him.

I worked all my life. I always had some type of stable employment. I expect Andre to be like me when he's twelve or thirteen. I'm the only boy out of six children.

A lot of men figure, if you're not going to let me see my child, I'm not going to pay child support. I figure you have to support your child. You made that child, even if you don't have visitation rights. Go to court to get visitation rights if that is what it takes. Anyway, you should pay support—at least that way you know you're doing your part.

The people who are making decisions to cut funding for programs that help young people should come and live here for a couple of years. They would realize that they shouldn't take out most of the programs they want to take out. There are some kids who don't want to be helped, but I think it depends on the person—whether you've had values instilled in you. I have seen people who graduated from high school, but they think: "I've been going to school getting A's all this time. I'm almost a grown man and I have no street experience." And they just want to hang out. Then, when they get too caught up in life on the street, they're gone.

I started out being one of the types who was getting straight A's, but then I wanted to see what was going on in the street. I started cutting, coming to school at 10:30, 11:00 AM. The school didn't care. They just made me leave day school after I started cutting classes. They told me that in order to get into night school, my mother had to come and sign me in. My mother came to sign me in and the teachers never showed up.

So I was spending my money to catch the bus there every night, and the teachers didn't show up. When they did show up they gave us crossword puzzles and stuff like that to do. I just stopped

Taking responsibility as a father means trying to spend more time with your child. This often means less time for socializing with friends.

going. Then when my son was born, I switched over to taking care of him.

I tried to get steady work. I got work as a utility guy, but they tried to take advantage of me. If I got sick they wouldn't give me time off. If I had to go to court about child support or if Andre was sick, they never gave me the time off. They told me if I didn't show up, my job would be at stake. So they laid me off during the summer and I'm hoping to find another job before the fall.

Some young men only want to get into a girl's drawers. If they don't want to be with that girl, at least they got what they wanted. Then they say, "See you later."

Feeding and cleaning are some of the day-to-day tasks of parenting.

If you're not willing to give yourself up for your kids, you shouldn't have any. Your child will always come first. I had a problem with that at first; I let my girlfriend do everything. Then my girlfriend told me, "This is as much your child as it is mine." Then I started taking him out, giving him baths, and feeding him, and I found I really liked it.

I think my son realizes I'm his father. He respects his mom even though he's only one year old. If he doesn't do something his mom tells him, I just give him that look and he slouches down in his seat. I think he knows when he does something wrong.

My son also knows I'm going to be there for him. I didn't have that with my dad. He always thought I wanted the street life, so I had to prove to him that's not what I wanted.

Teens should enjoy their lives while they can. My girlfriend was my first and I was her first, and having a baby just happened.

I believe the younger generation doesn't want to understand the responsibilities involved in having a family.

MICHAEL IS NINETEEN YEARS OLD. HE HAS A one-year-old son, Cain Michael, with his girlfriend Jessica. They are expecting a second child.

Both Michael and Jessica live and work in the Minneapolis/St. Paul area. Michael earned his GED at the Family and Community Educational Services, which is part of the Minneapolis Department of Public Schools. He is hoping to continue his education by studying law enforcement at a local college.

2 MICHAEL— Learning About Responsibility

I WAS SEVENTEEN WHEN **C**AIN WAS CONCEIVED AND eighteen when he was born. My girlfriend, Jessica, had a miscarriage the first time she got pregnant. When Cain was conceived, my mom asked me, "Are you ready for it?" I said, "Well, I'm as ready as I'm ever going to be." She was behind me 100 percent.

My girlfriend's adoptive mother just freaked out. She had heard a lot of rumors about how I was some kind of gangster, and I guess she believes them. She doesn't know me at all. She won't even take the time to talk to me.

Now that we're having a second child, Jessica's mom's attitude toward her is: This is the stupidest thing you've ever done. I'm Native American and Jessica's white. Jessica's mom says I'm going to be a fat, lazy drunk, and I'm going to beat her and beat my son. That's not the case at all. My girlfriend and her mother are kind of getting through it, and her mom is kind of accepting the situation the way it is, I guess. Her mom helps with food and stuff for the baby, but she wouldn't give anything to help me. My mom gives help to all three of us.

I was there at the birth. It wasn't like what everybody said it would be. Jessica only went through three hours of labor—it was fairly fast. When she went into the hospital, they measured her; she was already dilated six centimeters. They put her on something that sped up her labor. The baby came rather quickly. I was kind of prepared for it and kind of not. I didn't know what to expect. What I saw on videos about birth really scared the heck out of me—there were women who went through nineteen, forty-eight hours of labor.

When Jessica was pregnant, she was eating as much as I was. I had never seen Jessica eat that much! But I figured she was eating for two. Then I gained weight too. She lost it quicker than I did though.

I got yelled at a lot for little stuff when Jessica was pregnant, but I kind of expected that. She was really grumpy and crabby. "Don't touch me," she would say. When Cain was born, I forgot all of that. I was watching my son, and he wasn't even crying— he was looking at me. It made me a lot happier, especially since it was something I didn't expect. It made me love him. I can see that he can finally show affection for me now that he's one year old.

When we brought Cain home, I went through a stage of thinking: "I don't want to drop him, I might break him." I didn't get to hold my brothers and sisters very much, so I didn't know what it was like to hold a baby.

I work for Federal Express loading planes at Minneapolis Airport. I didn't finish high school before Cain was born. I didn't do well in the twelfth grade so I gave up on it and worked full time. Then I went to the Family and Community Educational Services in Minneapolis and got my GED. I figured I had better do something with my life. Otherwise I'm going to stay in the same place and I don't want to do that. I found jobs before I got my GED, but mostly a lot of manual labor. Now that I have the GED it's making things a little easier. Plus I just went to get financial aid to continue my schooling. I'm trying to go to a community law enforcement college. I want to become a sheriff.

At first I wanted to be a paramedic or something like that. Then I started to read more about law enforcement and I thought that sounded interesting. My best friend's parents are both in law enforcement, and they've told me a lot about it.

Jessica's working too. We're doing a trade-off right now. She's working in the morning and I'm working in the evening. We get to see each other now and then. It's kind of hard, and it's going to

How you feel about your own childhood can have an effect on your experience as a father.

make the relationship a little bit hard, but it's been working out.

I didn't expect all the bills. And when Cain gets sick I don't know what to do. I never took care of my sisters and brothers that way. I helped raise them while my mom was doing her schooling. I took care of their diapers and stuff, so I kind of knew what to do—except for the sick part. I don't have my mom here all the time. She usually knows what to do.

Of course I want Cain to do better than I have so I'm trying to save up all the money I can so he doesn't have to worry about getting financial aid for college. I want to make sure he gets good enough schooling. My mom did that for me.

My brother Matthew is close to my age; he's sixteen. He's talked to me about sex a few times. He pretty much knew what was going on, but I told him, "Make sure you're using birth control. Being a father may sound cool and stuff, but it really brings a lot of responsibility. You're sixteen—you're probably not ready for it. You may be, you may not be, but it's better to wait than take the chance and do it. It's just a lot of responsibility that you're going to put on yourself." Matthew tends to listen to me; we talk every now and then.

Having a baby has made me a lot more responsible. It's made me see there's more than just me to take care of. When Cain gets to be a teenager, I'll tell him what I know. I want him to wait to have sex. It's going to be his decision though.

If you're going to be having sex, it's going to put a lot of responsibility on you that you don't need. You need to get through school; you need to get certain things taken care of before you have children, because you're just a kid yourself. I'm still young, but I put the responsibility on myself, and I'm going to stick with it until the day I die.

I'd tell kids to be really careful. I know a lot of guys out there who don't care who they're with. I tell them they should be real selective because later they will find out they have herpes or gonorrhea and they will think to themselves they shouldn't have done it. Well, you should be a little more careful about who you choose.

I have a lot of friends who have children. My friends love their children. I see it every time we are together. We love each other's children as if they were our own. We're all on tough schedules—everything has to be perfectly timed with the babies and our work. We've tried to talk to younger teenagers about being fathers. I think young teenagers should know what they're getting into. It is a lot of responsibility—I can't say that enough. If they want to do it, it's not the easiest thing in the world. It's worth it to me—I love my son. He looks just like me and I love the way he smiles at me. I love everything he does.

I think it's hard for kids when they grow up without fathers in the family. It was for me. I had certain questions about things that were hard to go to my mom with, and I wanted to have a man's opinion. My stepfather's attitude was, "You're not my kid, but I love your mother." I didn't like him too much, and he didn't like me. For me it's important to be in my son's life. I want him to know who his father is. I want him to know that I'm going to be there for the rest of my life. If he needs anything, even if it's 2:00 AM and he has a flat tire or something, I want him to know I'm going to be there for him.

My father was a big drinker. I went to live with him twice, and it didn't work out. I didn't even get to know who he was, and I left on bad terms.

There are a lot of fathers who have gotten bad reputations over the years because of stuff like that. A girl gets pregnant, and right away the family thinks, "Well, when is he going to leave you?" or "I know he's not going to be around, I've seen it before." Well, you may have seen it before, but that doesn't mean *I'm* going to do it.

Some young men want to stay with their kids. Others think, "I can leave when my girlfriend gets pregnant. If it happens, oh, well." They're just going to brush it off—I've seen that. For me, that's my flesh and blood, and I take my family very seriously. I want to show my son that I'm going to be there, that he's loved, and that I'm not like some of those fathers.

I'm trying to make it so that more teenage fathers really get looked at for who they are rather than being automatically shunned. People think that because a guy is young he's going to leave his girlfriend and his kid. I don't want it to be that way, because my friends are good fathers. I see it every time I look at them. And I'm in for the long haul no matter what.

ZACHARY IS NINETEEN YEARS OLD. HE LIVES IN St. Paul, Minnesota, with his girlfriend and their fourteen-month-old daughter. He graduated from high school.

Zachary has talked to many reporters about young fatherhood because he wants society to know that "We're not all deadbeat dads. Some of us are trying hard to do what's right."

3 ZACHARY— A Daughter Is Very Special

I HAVE A DAUGHTER, MARYAH, WHO IS FOURTEEN months old. I was eighteen when she was born. My girlfriend, Rachael, and I met as sophomores in a private Catholic school. We started going out when we were both juniors. We did our little bit of partying and hanging out. I got along with her friends, and she got along with mine. It was comfortable and free.

Rachael wants to get married. I don't know if I'm ready. I'm playing it by ear. I'm more ready to be a father than a husband. I'm not sure why. I think it's the other big "C" word—commitment. I know that I love her, and I'm sure I'll love her down the road. I also know that people change, and the divorce rate is really high. When I get married, it's going to be that one and only for the rest of my life. I want to make sure that I'm ready for it—that we're ready for it.

When Rachael got pregnant, it was a big surprise. We were using condoms, but they obviously didn't work. My mom, when I told her, was kind of quiet, but she didn't get mad. She got a little sad. Her dreams for me had changed suddenly, but she was very supportive. My father was sort of supportive. He was kind of pushing for adoption because his dreams for me weren't going the way he wanted them to. But he also understood that I needed to do what I needed to do. He said, "You're eighteen, technically you're your own man, and you have to make the decision."

Rachael's mother had died before I met her. Her father, who's kind of a conservative guy, said to Rachael, "Well, you're eating badly, so you better take your vitamins now." And that was pretty much it. We have very good relationships with both families. They're very supportive now.

My dad wanted me to live life like any other eighteen-year-old college guy—live in a dorm, do all that stuff. I wanted to do that too. But from the moment Rachael told me she was pregnant, I knew that would have to change. I didn't look at it in a bad way. It was time to take responsibility, so that's what I did. I'm going to community college now. It's a little different from what I had planned, but it's something that fits into my schedule now. I can take night classes and work full time. I'm sent to different businesses to work with their files, labeling and organizing them.

It's not fun work, but it helps pay the bills.

I'm taking general courses now. I was planning on going into law enforcement, but as I took a closer look it didn't fit me. I wanted to go out there and—a naive thought—"change the world." Our society's going downhill, the crime rate is going up, and I wanted to do my part. I wanted to be part of the solution. But I figured I'd be way too stressed out all the time because crime is a never-ending cycle. It would also be too stressful on Rachael and probably on Maryah, when she got older, to wonder whether they'd see me at dinnertime.

The birth was interesting for me, to say the least. The contractions started around noon when we were in school. We were doing laps around the building to get the contractions to speed up. At ten o'clock at night, the contractions were about five minutes apart, so we went to the hospital. I was kind of hoping this was going to be it. You hear stories about people who get their hopes up and then it turns out to be false labor or something.

They gave Rachael an epidural (a particular type of painkiller) that night to settle her down because the contractions got really painful. The next morning they said to her, "We're going to let you rest some more." I went down to have some breakfast with my mom at the hospital. They said, "Come back in an hour and we'll deliver the baby." So that's what happened. It was kind of awkward and kind of neat at the same time.

It was the best moment of my life. There had been all that waiting and anticipation for that very moment. I couldn't believe that it was actually here. I kept thinking I was dreaming.

The best part of having Maryah is everything. She's the most gorgeous little baby in the whole world. She has the most beautiful blue eyes, and she's starting to walk around now and she's talking a lot.

Rachael and I weren't living together when Maryah was born. We just moved this April into our own place. Rachael was living with her dad, 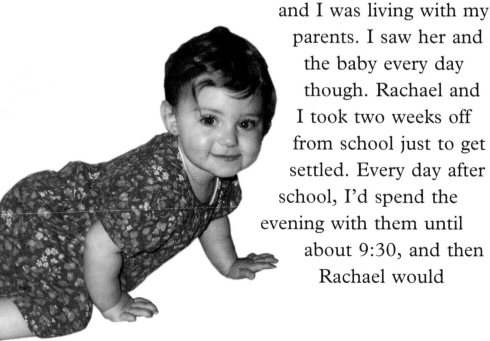 and I was living with my parents. I saw her and the baby every day though. Rachael and I took two weeks off from school just to get settled. Every day after school, I'd spend the evening with them until about 9:30, and then Rachael would

Maryah

drop me off, and we would do the same thing the next day.

I had experience changing diapers because I had two younger brothers. I did plenty of changing diapers with them. I was very comfortable with all of that. I love being a dad. Sometimes I wonder how my life could have been if I hadn't become a father at such a young age. If I had to do it again, I'd probably wait a couple of years until I was out of college.

I really don't know how younger kids who have kids manage to get along. I haven't fully matured myself, and I'm having a tough time with money. That's what Rachael and I usually argue about. I try to mellow out and live responsibly with money, but Rachael tends to be more uptight than I'd like her to be. But she sees that things can happen, like the car will break down and you'll have to fork out a couple of hundred dollars to fix it.

Rachael works full time too. We found a woman who provides excellent day care not too far from here, and she's not too expensive. Maryah loves it there. There are a couple of kids her age, or maybe a little older.

I worry and have nightmares about what Maryah's life will be like when she gets older. I see what's out there on the streets—how life is. My father and I live very different lives. He's very naive

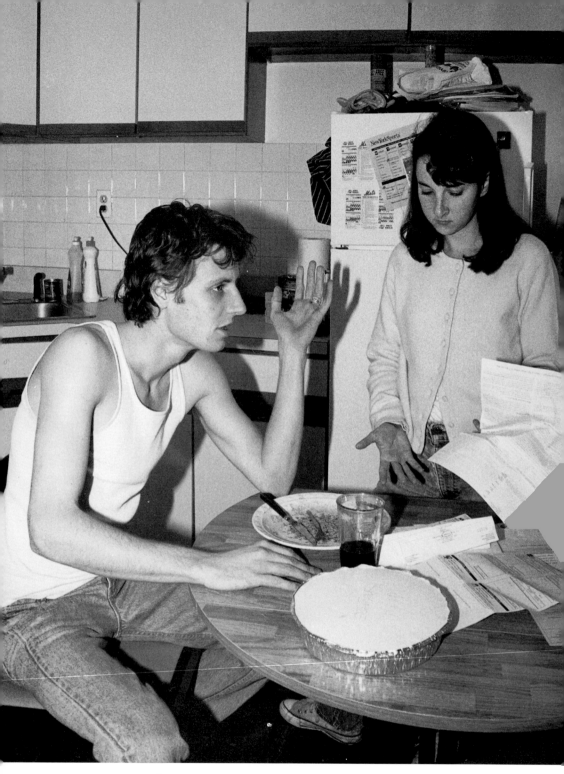

The financial burden of raising a child can put strain on a relationship.

about how life can be. I don't want Maryah to be naive, but I don't want her to feel all the pressures that a lot of people feel, either.

I have thought about what will happen when Maryah is interested in sex. I've thought about it a lot, and I really don't know what I'll do. I'm hoping that time and experience will bring me an answer. It really is a hard one. No matter which way I go on that issue, it's kind of like a dead end for me, because if I say, "Oh no, don't do that," then she's going to ask, "Well, what about you?"

STDS scare me, especially AIDS, because there's no cure. Maryah getting pregnant would scare me too. I see me having sex, and that's okay; but with her, I see it as a parent. This is what I have a lot of problems with. I'll look at a situation one way, but being a parent too, I'll see the other side of it. I'm nineteen years old, and I'm not going to be responsible all the time. But now I have to be because of the baby.

A teacher once said to us, "Next time that you ask a lady to go to bed with you, instead of saying, 'Let's go have sex,' say, 'Let's go make a baby,' and see if that makes a difference." It made sense to me because if kids are going to do something, they're going to do it, and they're going to tune out everything that's not what they want to do. Something about the way the teacher said that just clicked. I knew that condoms weren't 100-percent effective, but I thought it wouldn't happen to me.

I don't mind talking to people about this. I want to set a positive example. People come to me and say, "Good job for sticking by your girlfriend and your baby." They give me all sorts of support, which is good. They look at me as special, but why? This is what I *should* be doing. Society says, "A nineteen-year-old father? He's not going to stick around"—but you should. You have to. My friends who have children have been very good. They've all stuck around with their kids and partners. One of my friends, though, isn't very much in his son's life, and I lost a lot of respect for him because of that. He's still a kid. I'm still a kid too, but at least I try to see what's important and do my part in raising my child. He figured, "Oh, she'll take the baby, and I can go out and do whatever I want."

If Rachael had been a one-night stand, I still would have wanted to keep the baby, but I would have felt really guilty doing that to Maryah or another baby.

It is very hard, but we're making it. Trying to have enough time to be with Rachael and Maryah is very hard. When school starts back up, I'm going to be in school full time and working full time, and I'm not going to see them as much as I'd like to. Besides the weekends, I'm not going to have much time with Maryah or Rachael. I'll see them every day, but not for very long. It's hard, but it's something I need to do. I need to get through college so I can get a better-paying job. Then we can be more comfortable, and Maryah can get the education I didn't have.

ALFRED IS SEVENTEEN YEARS OLD, AND HE HAS a two-year-old son, Joshua Michael. While Alfred and his son's mother are not together and don't plan to marry, Alfred believes it will always be important for him to be in his son's life. Alfred is part of the Young Fathers' Program at the Valley, an organization that helps teens.

4 ALFRED— Getting to Know Your Son

I'VE KNOWN MY GIRLFRIEND FOR ABOUT FOUR YEARS now. I was fourteen and she was sixteen when she got pregnant. We wanted to be together, but we didn't plan the baby. We weren't using birth control.

My family was happy about the baby but they were worried about the fact that we were so young. They were worried about my future. My girl-friend's parents were really mad because she was so young, but they learned to accept that we were going to have a baby.

I was there at the birth. I couldn't be in the delivery room because of my age. I stayed in the waiting room, pacing back and forth. It was about a four-hour wait.

Joshua's mother and I are not together, but we're good friends right now. We work at communication and understanding.

I got kicked out of school because of a big conflict, and I was just laying around the house not doing anything. Then I saw an advertisement for the Valley over at the Young Adults' Learning Center. I decided that I had to stop being lazy and go out there to get some job training and to further my education. I've been at the Valley's program about six months.

During my time at the Valley, I found out about the Young Fathers' Program. I learned a lot. I learned that having a baby is not all about money. It's more about how I spend time with him. I love my son, and I spend as much time as I can with him. I take him to the park, to the zoo. Sometimes he comes over to my house and I teach him little words, the alphabet, and numbers. I take him to the park and play with him—we run around.

I'm going to court right now to get visitation rights. Joshua's mother's parents think I shouldn't see Joshua because I can't give them money. I just started working at an internship with the Valley. They thought I did really well, so they gave me a full-time job. I'm willing to pay whatever I can to help support Joshua. From the courts, I'll get a set payment to make so I won't have to jump from giving them $100 one time and then dropping back to $50. I'm willing to make the set payment.

Having a son, I just can't go out there and get a $100 pair of sneakers for myself. I have to get things for my child—the baby clothes or whatever

It can be difficult to pursue educational goals while raising a baby.

he needs. I didn't think about it much before I had the baby. I didn't think it was going to change my life, but it did.

I'm hoping that when Joshua gets older he'll understand me and where I'm coming from. I hope he knows that if I can't get him something I'll still be there for him. I don't know now what I'll say to him when he gets to the point where he wants to have sex. I hope by that time I'll be prepared to break it down for him.

My life has been good since Joshua was born. I stopped hanging out. Before, I was selfish and greedy. So I tell other young men to open up their eyes, and I let them know that if they're going to have sex, to have it safely. And I let them know that if they're going to have a baby they should have it with the right girl . . . a girl you can be with for the rest of your life. And make sure you have some education to get a good job before you mess up and go out there and have a baby at a young age.

It's hard to grow up without a dad. It was hard for me growing up knowing my mother had to do everything. My father wasn't really there. My father is starting to come back into my life. It's wonderful now, but I ask him, "Why do you want to come into my life now when you weren't there before?" I wanted to accept him in my life with no problems. He hasn't told me why he wasn't there, but my mother told me he couldn't deal with the stress of being a father. The money was hard for him to get. If my father had been in my life earlier, I might have had safer sex, used protection, and made sure she had protection. Young men should make sure they have safe sex, because AIDS is affecting everybody.

My life is harder now with Joshua. I can't stop anybody from having sex, but I would advise them to have safe sex and that if they have a baby to be there for the baby, not only financially but emotionally and physically. Joshua knows who his mother is and who his father is. He also knows we're not together now.

I hope that Joshua finishes school and that when he's ready to have a baby he has it with the right girl. I want Joshua to be very successful in life, to go to college, to get a degree, to make a nice home for himself. I want the same things for myself. I'll be taking my GED test in August, and then I hope to go to college. I'd like to study human resources and become a counselor.

JOHN HAD HIS FIRST SON WHEN HE WAS fifteen years old and his girlfriend was fourteen. In the past eight years, they have married and had two more children.

John is now actively involved in working with other young men who have children at a community-based program in New York City.

5 JOHN— Making a Life for a Family of Five

I HAVE THREE CHILDREN, EIGHT YEARS OLD, FIVE years old, and fourteen months old. I have two sons and a daughter. I was fifteen when my first son was born. My wife and I were in junior high school together. We had been dating for about a year and a half. We had not planned on starting a family at that age. She was thirteen when she got pregnant. It was hard at fifteen finding out you're going to be a father and you're still a child your-self. I just grabbed the bull by the horns and rode it through.

Both sides of the family were upset because we were so young. They knew that our lives would change dramatically, but they were there for us 110 percent.

It was tough. I didn't know what to expect from my girlfriend, and I didn't know what to give to her. She didn't know what to expect from me or what I was supposed to offer either. We were both new at this. When she asked me, "Am I gaining a

lot of weight?" was I supposed to say, "Yeah"? My
brother told me you're supposed to say no, never
tell her she's gaining weight when she's pregnant. I
learned a lot with the first baby.

People have to understand that when a woman
is pregnant, a man is pregnant too. I definitely was.
Especially with the last one—I put on forty
pounds. I ate everything there was to eat. If it
wasn't chained down I ate it. My moods would
change, too. I bonded with my wife. The minute
she said she was pregnant I bonded, and then I
bonded with the baby.

I went to the hospital, but I didn't go into the
labor room because I was really nervous and
scared. My wife was only in labor for a couple of
hours with my first son. My daughter took the
longest—four days.

The feeling I had when I first saw the baby is so
hard to describe—you can't put it into words. It's
such a natural high. It's so dramatic and so touch-
ing. I know I only get that feeling when my children are born, no other time.

I was nervous and scared when my wife brought
the baby home. I was hoping everything would be
all right. I was really gentle with the baby. It was
an experience helping to take care of the baby. I
just got out of diapers not too long ago and now I
had to change someone else's.

I stayed in school. I went on to high school but then I dropped out when my second son was born. I just kept working and working, then went back and took my GED. I went to college for a semester, then left. I plan to go back to college. I've been working at the community-based program for about two years now.

At the program we learn a lot of things. The first thing I learned was that it's a blessing to be a father. Not many people have the opportunity to be fathers. You have to do what you're supposed to be doing, and be out there working, going to school, trying to better your life so your children have a better life.

I married my partner two years ago. And she got pregnant with my daughter just after we got married. We enjoy having our kids.

My wife stayed home with the children at first. Now she's in college and doing great. My wife is very supportive. She told me to get myself together and make sure I got on the ball. We've been through some rough times.

Having a child is nothing that should be done just for the fun of it or because you need someone to love you unconditionally. It has a mental and emotional effect on you. It's something that's going to be very hard—you have this life in your hands.

Don't just worry about getting a girl pregnant, though. There are also diseases out there. There's AIDS and STDS. Sex is something very emotional and personal. You're sharing yourself with someone. You want to make sure that the person you're sharing yourself with is special. You're giving away your body. You want to make sure you want to be with that person.

By who you are and what you do, you create a legacy. You can create a negative legacy by doing things that are not right and by doing things without morals or values. So why not create a positive legacy instead? I want to live on through my grandchildren and great-grandchildren. I want them to say, "My grandfather, John, had a set of values. He was very successful. Times were rough and he stuck it out." You want your legacy to live on with your whole family. I could be dead for 100 years and I still want them to be telling stories of the things I did.

My mother raised me in a single-parent home because my father chose not to be there. I learned from that experience and what my mother taught me. It's hard to grow up without a father. But what I came to learn is that if you don't have a father there, you can learn from that experience. Your father can be in your home and not be there for you, too. A lot of kids know what it's like not to have a father there for you. You can decide you do not want to do that to your child.

I've been very committed to being a father since my oldest son was born. I know I was put here on this earth to do something extremely positive. You've got to condition yourself and discipline yourself and believe in yourself. Things will get rough, but what's good about my family is that they're supportive.

Not all young men feel that way. They want to be good fathers, but they don't know how.

Society has this disdain for young fathers as "hit-and-run artists," just wanting to be with any woman and making enough babies to have two football teams. That's not true. People see me with my three children. They see me picking up my children from school. They see me in the park with my children. They see me raising my children and they have to think about the things they read in the papers or in a book about how young fathers don't care for their children.

For every young man it's different. I know a lot of young men have different issues around their children. It's not always true that young fathers don't want to be with their children. It could be that there are conflicts between the father and the mother, or between him and her family. Everybody's situation has different dynamics. There are some forces that keep young fathers away from their children. If the program can change my life, it can definitely change anybody's life. The staff at the program is on the front line dealing with these young dads, assessing the situation, helping them. You have to get your hands dirty and see how you can change people's lives. It's like war.

Daezon

I have seen a lot of changes since I was twelve and thirteen. I see a lot of things twelve- and thirteen-year-olds have to worry about now, like not having a bus pass to get to school, like having moms and dads who don't have enough money to give them lunch money. Now the kids twelve and thirteen years old have to worry about whether they're going to eat lunch. Now survival is getting hard.

Justin

Niquasha

It's a myth that all young fathers don't want to take care of their responsibilities and don't want to be there. If you get a young guy who's fifteen, who has no job training or no community-based organization to help him or keep him motivated to be in school and to teach him how to be a father, then of course he's going to feel bad. Because society says that if you're a father, you have to come up with a certain amount of dollars. He's going to feel that he's bad and that he's not worthy of being a father if he can't come up with that money.

It's not all about money, though. My children are going to miss me and remember me because of all the time we spend together and because of all the things we do. They're not going to say, "Oh, I miss Daddy because I need these sneakers."

My daughter's the youngest so I hold her more, but now I have to spread that out. I put her down and pick up my youngest son, then I put him down and hold my oldest son. They demand time. Sometimes my wife gets jealous because there's just work and my children in my life. My time is so divided. It's not really a problem, it's more like a joke with us. She'll say, "Oh, you're at work and then you're playing with the children. When do you and I have time?"

We need things like community-based organizations to teach things to young fathers. It's like with a child. When that child is born you have to teach it things. You can't wait until it's eight or nine years old and then suddenly want to put values into that child. It's the same with young fathers: You have to teach us and grow with us and guide us. If society wants to run away from us now, when it's our turn to control things, what will happen? It's like giving a baby a loaded gun. What do you expect a baby to do? If you don't empower us, all you're doing is hurting yourself in the long run.

It seems strange now, but when I was twelve I didn't think about the future. I was thinking about going to school and playing baseball. Now I have to think about how I'm going to get to school and how I'm going to eat. That's why you have to have mentoring programs and men's rites of passage programs and things like that. Two years ago, I wouldn't have been able to talk like this, but after being in the program, I've learned how to speak and voice my opinion in a positive way.

You might know how it feels to not know your father. So when you have a relationship with a woman and you have a child, you can say, "You know what, I'm not hitting the door. When things get hard, I'm not hitting the door." You need a place where you can go to see positive males doing positive things. And the media needs to stop

Children need guidance and support from their parents.

portraying teen dads negatively. They need to know there are positive people out there.

Communities have to start caring about the youth and the kids. When you see the positive things the youth can do, that's important. When you help a youth, you're not only affecting the youth. You have youth who are parents, and you're affecting their children too. It's a domino effect. So it will affect you too.

I want my kids to experience a lot of things: growing up, being able to make decisions, and being able to make choices. I want them to be able to go into places without people thinking they're going to do something bad. I want my kids to experience the finer things in life.

Epilogue

THE FIVE TEEN FATHERS IN THESE STORIES HAVE learned a lot since becoming fathers, and they have a lot of lessons to teach us. Kenyatta has learned about the economic sacrifices involved in raising children. Michael deals with the difficulties of continuing his education. Zachary has learned about the difficulties of making a commitment to his relationship with his girlfriend. Alfred is still struggling to get visitation rights. John is learning how to give enough attention to all of his kids. Many of the fathers share some hard memories and experiences; some of their own fathers, for example, were not around for their childhoods.

Perhaps the most important lesson we can learn from these stories goes back to the beginnings of each father's situation: At a very young age, they had sex and got a young girl pregnant. That was the first choice they made in this process, and they have had to live with the consequences ever since.

Fatherhood is difficult for anyone at any age, but it is especially hard for teenagers, who are still learning about the world and their place in it. Suddenly there is a tiny baby, fragile, hungry, crying, and needy. Suddenly there is no time to watch movies, play a ball game, or hang out with your friends. Suddenly there are bills and responsibilities to deal with. Suddenly you have to deal not only with your homework or even your full-time job, but also with a full-time life as a father. Suddenly your girlfriend is not just someone you flirt with or see at school, but your partner in day-to-day decisions and crises.

The five fathers you met in this book can tell you a great deal about those changes and more. Thanks to their girlfriends or wives, families, friends, community organizations, and counselors, these young fathers have taken steps to build new lives for themselves and their families. Having kids has not meant the end of their lives. In fact, even in their teens, these young men have already discovered the joys as well as the difficulties of being fathers. With hard work and support from their families and others, they will be able to pursue their educations and dreams in the future.

All of them have learned that becoming a father does not automatically make you a man. They also know that it does force you to grow up, sooner than you might have wanted to.

Glossary

AIDS (Acquired Immunodeficiency Syndrome)
An incurable disease of the human immune system caused by infection with the Human Immuno-deficiency Virus (HIV).

assumption An idea or statement that is taken for granted to be true.

attitude A feeling, opinion, or idea about someone or something.

commitment Promising to do something in the future.

deadbeat One who fails to pay debts or expenses.

discipline Self-control.

GED (General Equivalency Diploma) A certificate earned when the recipient has passed coursework equivalent to a high school education.

involvement The state of taking part in and being committed to something.

legacy Something passed on from an ancestor.

male-hostile Something that is opposed to males; anti-male.

out-of-wedlock birth A birth that occurs when the parents are not married.

shunned Rejected.

STDS (sexually transmitted diseases) Diseases spread through sexual contact.

sterility Inability to bear children.

values Strong beliefs about what is important.

Help List

In the United States:

National AIDS Hotline
(800) 342-2437

National Campaign to Prevent Teen Pregnancy
2100 M Street NW, #300
Washington, DC 20037

National Center for Fatherhood
P.O. Box 41388
Kansas City, MO 64141
(800) 593-DADS [3237]

National Congress for Fathers and Children
(800) SEE-DADS [733-3237]

National Fatherhood Initiative
One Bank Street #160
Gaithersburg, MD 20878
(301) 948-0599

National Institute for Responsible Fatherhood
8555 Hough Avenue
Cleveland, OH 44106
(216) 791-1468

Planned Parenthood Federation of America
810 Seventh Avenue
New York, NY 10019
(212) 541-7800
E-mail: communications@ppfa.org
Web site: http://www.ppfa.org/ppfa/

In Canada:

Crisis Pregnancy Center
300-2445 13th Avenue
Regina, SK S4P 0W1
(306) 757-3356
http://www.cableregina.com/nonprofits/cpcregina/index.
    html

Planned Parenthood Federation of Canada
1 Nicholas Street, Suite 430
Ottawa, Ontario K1N 7B7
(613) 241-4474

For Further Reading

Aitkens, Maggie. *Kerry, A Teenage Mother.* Minneapolis, MN: Lerner Publications Company, 1994.

Annie's Baby: The Diary of Anonymous, a Pregnant Teenager. New York: Avon Flare, 1998.

Arthur, Shirley M. *Surviving Teen Pregnancy: Your Choices, Dreams, and Decisions.* Buena Park, CA: Morning Glory Press, 1996.

Ayer, Eleanor. *Everything You Need to Know About Teen Fatherhood.* New York: The Rosen Publishing Group, 1993.

Bode, Janet. *Kids Still Having Kids: People Talk About Teen Pregnancy.* New York: Franklin Watts, 1993.

Doherty, Berlie. *Dear Nobody.* Hinesdale, PA: Beech Tree Books, 1994.

Edelson, Paula. *Straight Talk About Teenage Pregnancy.* New York: Facts on File, 1998.

Hughes, Tracy. *Everything You Need to Know About Teen Pregnancy.* New York: The Rosen Publishing Group, 1997.

Jamiolkowski, Raymond. *A Baby Doesn't Make the*

Man: Alternative Sources of Power and Manhood for Young Men. New York: The Rosen Publishing Group, 1997.

Lindsay, Jeanne Warren. *Your Baby's First Year: A Guide for Teenage Parents.* Buena Park, CA: Morning Glory Press, 1998.

_____. *Teen Dads: Rights, Responsibilities, & Joys.* Buena Park, CA: Morning Glory Press, 1993.

Stewart, Gail. *Teen Fathers.* San Diego, CA: Lucent Books, 1997.

Index

A

adoption, 30
adulthood, 6
AIDS, 8, 35, 43, 48

B

birth, 22, 31–32, 46
birth control, 7, 9, 25, 39

C

child support, 15, 17
choices, 6, 7, 9, 10, 55
community-based
    organizations/programs,
    44, 51, 56
college, 10
    community college, 23, 30
condoms, 8, 29–30, 36

D

day care, 33
deadbeat dads, 10, 28
divorce, 29

E

education, 12, 20, 24, 25, 37,
    40, 42, 43, 55, 56
epidural, 31

F

fathers, absent, 9, 26, 42–43,
    48
financial aid, 23, 24
financial responsibilities, of
    fathers, 9

G

GED (General Equivalency
    Diploma), 10, 12, 20, 23,
    43, 47
government programs, 16

L

labor, 22, 46
    contractions, 31
    false, 31
law enforcement, 20, 23, 31
legacy, 48

M

manual labor, 23
marriage, 13, 29, 38, 44
miscarriage, 21

N

night classes/school, 14, 16,
    17, 30

P
paramedic, 23
protection, 43

R
responsibility, 9, 19, 25, 26,
    30, 56

S
safe sex, 43
sheriff, 23
single-parent homes, 26–27,
    42–43, 48

STDs (sexually transmitted
    diseases) 8, 35, 48,
AIDS, 8, 35, 43, 47
gonorrhea, 25–26
herpes, 25–26

V
visitation rights, 15, 40, 55

Y
Young Fathers' Program, 38,
    40

About the Author
Margi Trapani is a freelance writer. She has worked in communications for seventeen years. For six years she has directed a program that provides the media with information on youth issues. Ms. Trapani lives in New Jersey.

Photo Credits
Cover by Guillermina de Ferrari; p. 18 by Yung-Hee Chia; p. 24 by Seth Dinnerman; all other photos by Guillermina de Ferrari.

Layout and Design
Erin McKenna